ROYAL YACHTING ASSOCIATION

Yachting is one of the safest leisure sporting activities and 99.9% of yachtsmen will never use their liferaft...

...however, if you are one of the unlucky few, your chances of survival will be greatly increased if you understand how to use the equipment and how to help yourself.

This handbook is designed to accompany the RYA's one day Sea Survival course.

For further information and a list of establishments running the course, contact the RYA at RYA House Ensign Way Hamble Southampton, Hampshire SO31 4YA Tel: 02380 604100

YOUR BOAT IS THE BEST LIFERAFT

DO NOT get into the liferaft unless the boat is about to sink and you have done everything possible to save it.

Try to stop water rushing in by stuffing mattresses, sails etc. into any damage.

Sea cocks may break off so keep softwood bungs attached to them ready to block the hole.

Forcing a piece of wood, however ill fitting, into a hole can reduce the volume of water coming in to a level which can be handled by a normal bilge pump.

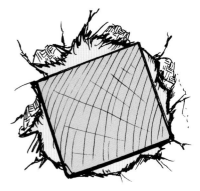

THE 1979 FASTNET RACE

303 yachts started this 605 mile race around the Fastnet Rock. At times the winds reached Force 11, but it was the confused seas that caused the damage.

A total of twenty-four yachts were abandoned of which only five sank. It easy to say that some crews abandoned too quickly, but each skipper had to make an extremely difficult decision based on the situation as he saw it at the time.

Tragically fifteen people lost their lives. Seven died after abandoning to their liferafts. Causes of death were drowning, exposure, or both.

THE ROBERTSON FAMILY

On 15 June 1972, 200 miles west of the Galapagos the 43ft wooden yacht *Lucette* was sunk by a killer whale. The Robertson family and a young friend survived for 38 days in a liferaft and later in their 9ft dinghy. Their book* relates how, in impossibly cramped conditions, they collected rain water, caught fish and turtles, administered brackish water enemas, while having to bail out their leaking liferaft and pump it up by mouth. They were finally rescued by a Japanese tunny boat who saw their flare.

THE BAILEYS

On 4 March 1973, Maurice and Marilyn Bailey were forced to abandon to their 4-man Avon liferaft and a nine foot inflatable after their 31ft yacht *Auralyn* was hit and sunk by a sperm whale some two hundred and fifty miles Northeast of the Galapagos. They spent 118 days drifting 1500 miles in their liferaft before being rescued by a Korean ship, the eighth vessel they had sighted.

The amazing success of their survival is down to their tremendous will to survive and their ability to improvise equipment. They lived mainly on raw fish, turtle meat and rain water**.

Today many ocean going yachtsmen carry a 406 MHz Emergency Position Indicating Radio Beacon. This piece of safety equipment, though not infallible, should reduce the chances of others having to go through similar ordeals to the Baileys and Robertsons.

Right: Maurice & Marilyn Bailey in Honolulu after their rescue by the Korean fishing boat Weolmi

* '*Survive the savage Sea*' Dougal Robertson (Sheridan House)
** '*118 Days adrift*' by Maurice & Marilyn Bailey (Nautical)

PREPARATION

SAFETY BRIEF

No matter how experienced your crew, a safety brief is essential. It should cover stowage and use of all safety equipment and should include the passage and pilotage plan for the day.

If anything should happen to you they would have at least some idea how to make a Mayday call on the radio and give a position!

THE VHF

Stick a MAYDAY prompt card in a prominent position next to the VHF and make sure your crew know how to switch on, select the distress channel and transmit a MAYDAY. Remember VHF sets vary from boat to boat.

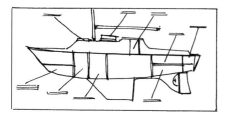

Labels clearly indicating where equipment is stowed will help reduce panic during an emergency.

First aid kit, Tools and spares, Fuel shut off, Emergency torches, Engine sea cock, Gas shut off, Flares, Grab bag, Dinghy.

THE LIFERAFT

Launching instructions should be on the liferaft canister. Make sure they are big enough to read without your specs!

Make sure the painter is correctly attached.

Northern European waters have excellent Search & Rescue (SAR) facilities. Devices which will help them locate you quickly are more important than a survival capsule that will keep you alive indefinitely.

FLARES

Flares are the simplest method of signalling distress. Parachute rockets are the most effective for raising the alarm, in perfect conditions they can be seen up to 40 miles away.

Rockets tend to 'Seek the wind' so for the highest possible trajectory they should be fired down-wind at an angle of about 15° to the vertical.

Hand-held pinpoint red flares also have an alarm-raising capability but their main purpose is to pinpoint the position of survivors or vessel in distress. They are most effective in the dark or in dull conditions.

Always hold a hand-flare downwind and clear of raft as hot molten ash spits from the end of the flare. BEWARE, if there is fuel on the water, the flare may set it alight. A handheld flare burns ⅔ rds way down the barrel and is extremely hot. DON'T look directly at the flare, it will damage your vision, particularly at night.

Orange smoke signals are more effective than red hand-held flares in bright sunlight. There are two types, hand-held which operate in the same way as hand-held flares and buoyant which are activated and then thrown overboard. The latter produce a much greater volume of smoke and burn for three times as long. A buoyant smoke signal should be thrown into the sea to leeward of the hull, where the smoke will tend to build up rather than disperse.

HELIOGRAPH

A signalling mirror is designed to attract the attention of ships and aircraft.

RAISING THE ALARM

BY RADIO

VHF, HF, MF radio or satellite communication, allow you to speak directly to a Rescue Co-ordination Centre or another vessel. Hence you can both call for help and know that your call has been received and help is on the way.

MAKING A MAYDAY CALL

MAYDAY is the international distress signal.

SWITCH ON THE RADIO – SELECT CHANNEL 16 – SELECT HIGH POWER.

PRESS TRANSMIT SWITCH AND SEND THE FOLLOWING MESSAGE:

MAYDAY – 3 times

YACHT NAME – 3 times

MAYDAY – YACHT NAME

POSITION – Either as latitude and longitude or as a range and bearing from a conspicuous and unambiguous charted object.

NATURE OF DISTRESS – Briefly, what the problem is, e.g. sinking, on fire, stranded.

ASSISTANCE REQUIRED – Usually just " Immediate assistance required."

SUPPLEMENTARY INFORMATION – Anything that may help rescuers such as the number of people on board or the fact that you are about to abandon to the liferaft.

OVER – The invitation to reply.

WAIT ONE MINUTE FOR A REPLY. IF NONE IS RECEIVED CHECK THAT THE BATTERIES ARE SWITCHED ON, THE SET IS SWITCHED ON, CHANNEL 16 AND HIGH POWER ARE SELECTED. REPEAT THE MAYDAY CALL.

IF THERE IS STILL NO REPLY, TRY ANOTHER CHANNEL (e.g. Ch6 or a working channel of the nearest coast radio station.)

Elementary mistakes, such as forgetting to turn on the set, can be made in an emergency, so make up a reminder card and stick it up near the radio.

The 'name' and the word 'yacht' helps the searchers know what they are looking for.

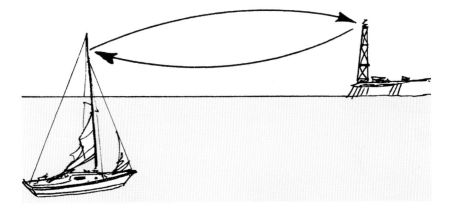

This format is internationally recognised and it is important to use it. Your distress call may be received by someone to whom English is a foreign language but if he receives the information in a format with which he is familiar he will understand it.

Take particular care with the position which you send. You may be able to read off Lat. and Long. direct from Decca or GPS. If you are using the range and bearing method there are a number of pitfalls to avoid. The convention is that you give bearing from and distance from the reference point, i.e. "My position is 150 degrees from Start Point Light, 15 miles". Make sure your reference point is unambiguous – there are five different rocks called Mewstone off the south coast of Devon and Cornwall so this would not be a good reference point to use.

MOBILE PHONES

Mobile phones have been known to work more than 40 miles offshore, but coverage is not guaranteed. Coastguard stations can direction find on VHF Ch16 and SAR units can home on a marine band radio signal but neither can direction find or home on a mobile phone signal. If a mobile phone is all you have available then dial 999 and ask for Coastguard – it may be better than nothing.

LOCATION

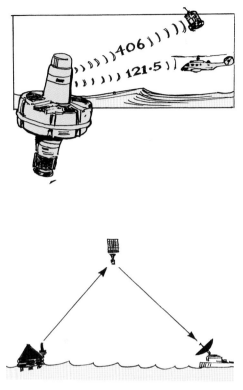

EPIRB (Emergency Position Indicating Radio Beacon)

An EPIRB sends a distress signal that initiates a co-ordinated rescue attempt. There are two basic types on the market; the 406MHz EPIRB and the 121.5MHz PLB (Personal Locator Beacon).

A 406MHz EPIRB can pin-point your position within 5 miles anywhere in the world. As well as transmitting signals on 406MHz for initial alert most beacons also transmit on 121.5MHz for homing by search units.

Once triggered the EPIRB transmits a signal to a COPAS/SARSAT orbiting satellite. This is relayed to a rescue co-ordination centre with identifying details of the beacon. SAR aircraft and helicopters are able to home in on the 121.5MHz signal.

The EPIRB's lithium battery needs to be replaced every 4-5 years, but once triggered it will transmit for 48 hours.

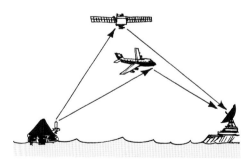

PLBs operate on the two aviation distress frequencies, 121.5MHz (Civil) and 243MHz (Military). Their signals can also be received by COPAS/SARSAT satellites but the satellite cannot store the signal, it simply re-transmits it. Hence they are effective through satellites only when the beacon and a satellite earth station are both within the satellite's horizon. Position finding by the satellite is much less accurate for a 121.5MHz signal than for a 406MHz signal.

There is a very high incidence of spurious signals on 121.5MHz so rescue co-ordination centres may not react to a single satellite detection on this frequency.

SARTS (Search And Rescue Transponders)

SARTS are relatively new devices carried on commercial vessels and aircraft.

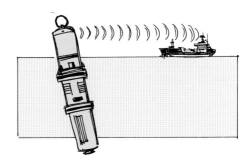

On receipt of a radar signal the transponder is activated and transmits a distinctive emergency signal on the radar screen. The main advantage of the SART is that signals can be picked up by all vessels and aircraft fitted with radar and not just those with specialist Search and Rescue equipment.

SAR units can home in on VHF and MF, but if you are using a hand held VHF in a liferaft its low aerial height and small power output means it will only transmit to your visible horizon. Save your batteries until you can see whoever you are trying to contact.

GMDSS (Global Maritime Distress and Safety System)

GMDSS is a new comprehensive world-wide distress communication system.

GMDSS divides the oceans of the world into sea areas, depending on the radio coverage.

A1   within VHF range of a coast radio station fitted with Digital Selective Calling (DSC).
A2   within MF range of a coast radio station fitted with DSC.
A3   within coverage of INMARSAT marine communication satellites.
A4   all other areas, such as polar regions, where the only communications coverage is HF.

The shore facilities required by GMDSS are now being installed and many are already operational. All merchant ships over 300 tons will have to be fitted with the GMDSS equipment for their operating area by February 1999.

Whilst there will be no legal requirement for yachts to fit GMDSS equipment it is likely that many will choose to do so. The main change will involve fitting equipment for Digital Selective Calling on VHF channel 70. This allows the transmission of a digital distress call giving the identity of the vessel in distress, her position and the nature of the distress. The message can be transmitted as a condensed data burst in about 0.5 seconds, the position and the time can be input direct from a GPS receiver and the boat's identity is pre-programmed into the DSC controller.

After an initial digital distress alert on channel 70, subsequent communication continues on channel 16 by voice.

LIFEJACKETS AND BUOYANCY AIDS

There should be one lifejacket for every member of the crew. They need to be checked and serviced regularly, especially the gas inflation types. There are different types, each designed for a specific purpose. The buoyancy rating, given in Newtons (N), with the equivalents in kilograms (kg), and pounds (lbs), is explained below.

All new lifejackets must have a CE mark which is the European replacement of the old BSI standard.

The relevant standards are:

BS/EN 393:1994 50 Newton Buoyancy Aid
BS/EN 395:1994 100 Newton Buoyancy Aid
BS/EN 396:1994 150 Newton Lifejacket
BS/EN 399:1994 150 Newton Lifejacket

A buoyancy aid is a flotation device that will help the wearer help himself in the water. They are comfortable to wear but are not recommended as life saving equipment. Often they look like padded waist coats or can be part of a sailing jacket.

A child's lifejacket has reduced buoyancy but the same buoyancy rating as an adult's, e.g. 50N and 150N. Many have harnesses and crutch straps built in as standard.

A 50N buoyancy aid (5kg or 11lbs) is designed to help support a competent swimmer in inshore waters where help is close at hand.

A 100N buoyancy aid (10kg or 22lbs) is suitable for competent swimmers for general inshore use. It is unlikely to self-right an unconscious person.

BEWARE - in some European countries 100N buoyancy aids may be sold as lifejackets.

LIFEJACKETS AND BUOYANCY AIDS

PUTTING ON A LIFEJACKET

You should be able to put your lifejacket on in less than a minute. Practice until you can.

Don't wait until an emergency arises before trying on your lifejacket.

If it's not properly fitted you can easily slip out of it once you're in the water.

Put waist strap through the highest setting on the back strap to pull collar of lifejacket down, this will help stop you slipping through.

The waist strap needs to be tight to the extent that it is almost uncomfortable. Lifejackets are almost impossible to adjust once you are in water.

Use the crotch strap if it's fitted.

A correctly fitted lifejacket with crotch straps will greatly increase the chances of survival.

Wearing oilskins, particularly if fitted with a hood will help to reduce heat loss and extend your survival time.

LIFEJACKETS AND BUOYANCY AIDS

OPTIONAL EXTRAS

1. Hood
2. Retro reflective tape
3. Twin chambers (275N)
4. Harness
5. Clip, used to attach yourself to other survivors in the water
6. Crotch strap
7. Light with a manual or salt water activated switch
8. Personal EPIRB, Whistle, Mini-flare pack
9. Manual inflation cord

LIFERAFTS

The liferaft is designed to help keep you alive for a limited period should your vessel sink. It also keeps you in the area of the abandonment so the rescue services are more likely to find you if you sent a distress signal before taking to the liferaft.

It is important that your liferaft is serviced annually by a reputable recognised service centre. A good centre will let you see your liferaft unpacked and inflated which gives you the chance to see what it looks like out of its pack.

Canopy may need supporting.

LEISURE RAFTS

These may be extremely basic, they are not manufactured to any national or international standard, and are not approved for any commercial operation. The raft is cheap, light in weight with minimal contents (no flares) but better than nothing. The canopy may not be automatically deployed, it may have to be put in place manually, and there is usually only one buoyancy compartment (puncture it and you are literally sunk).

Relies on single inflation tube

INFLATABLE ACTIVE SURVIVAL CRAFT

Some makes of inflatable active survival craft are approved by some offshore racing administrations but not by the Marine Safety Agency and there is no recognised standard for them. There is, however, something to be said for a survival craft which you can actively sail or row towards safety.

Blue water cruising sailors have often designed improvised lifeboats with the aim of having a survival craft in which they can effect their own rescue because some areas of the oceans have minimal rescue facilities.

LIFERAFTS

ORC LIFERAFTS

These rafts are manufactured to the Offshore Racing Council specification for yacht liferafts. There is, however, no system for independent inspection and certification of the rafts.

It is the type of liferaft most likely to be carried by the average yacht.

The specification is very similar to the DoT approved rafts (see below) and calls for at least two buoyancy compartments, either one of which could support the number of people the raft is designed to carry. Note that this does not mean that the intact raft can carry twice the rated capacity, it does not have enough room. Other important aspects of the specification include adequate floor area, sufficient water ballast pockets and an automatically erecting canopy.

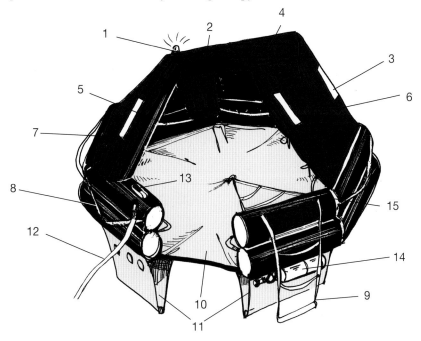

1.	Automatically activated light	10.	Floor (may have inflatable option)
2.	Lookout port	11.	Water pockets – increase stability
3.	Retro reflective tape		and reduce drift
4.	Auto inflation canopy arch	12.	Painter
5.	Grab straps/lines	13.	Safety knife
6.	Orange canopy	14.	CO_2 inflation gas cylinder
7.	Tied back door (quick release)	15.	Straps for pulling yourself on
8.	Lifelines		board
9.	Weighted ladder		

DEPARTMENT OF TRANSPORT APPROVED LIFERAFTS

For a liferaft to be Department of Transport approved it must have been manufactured to a design approved by the DoT and built in a factory which is subject to inspection by the Department. There are two grades of DoT approved rafts, SOLAS and non-SOLAS. The SOLAS rafts comply in all respects with the Safety of Life at Sea Convention of the International Maritime Organisation.

The SOLAS specification covers all aspects of design and construction. It is a rigorous specification, including parameters such as capability to withstand damage when stowed in air temperatures between -30°C to +60°C or when dropped into the water from a height of 18 metres. The smallest size of liferaft permitted by the SOLAS standard is 6 persons, and all must have an inflatable floor.

Non-SOLAS rafts are built to slightly reduced standards, for instance the coldest stowage temperature is -18°C and the drop height is reduced to 6 metres. The smallest size available is 4 person and the inflatable floor is not compulsory.

The higher the specification of the raft, the more it costs. A full SOLAS specification liferaft is likely to be 60% more expensive than the same size of ORC raft and more than twice the price of a leisure raft.

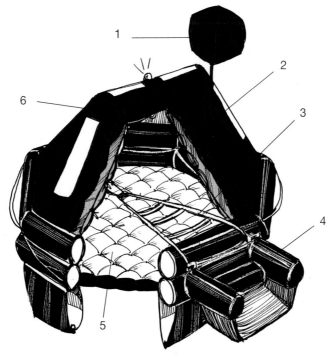

1. Inflatable radar reflector	5. Inflatable floor
2. Double canopy	6. Instructions printed on inside of
3. Straps to help pull you in	canopy
4. Inflatable ramp	

LIFERAFT STOWAGE

Ideally the liferaft should be stowed
where it is immediately accessible and
protected from heavy weather. These
two requirements are mutually
contradictory so a compromise is
needed.

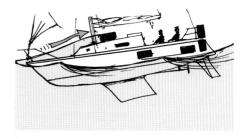

Rafts can be deck-mounted on the
coachroof. Alternatively they can be
kept in a special locker in the cockpit or
at the stern or fixed in a bracket on the
pushpit.

Any water ingress during normal storage may damage the cylinder, flares and first
aid kit causing damage to the raft itself.

HYDROSTATIC RELEASE UNITS – HRUs

If there is insufficient time to launch the
liferaft manually an HRU automatically
releases it when submerged 1-4 metres
under water. The raft floats to the
surface, inflates and detaches from the
craft as it sinks.

They are available as a cheap unit with
a two-year lifespan or a more expensive
type which can be serviced.

SAFETY CHECKS

Ensure the painter is attached to the
HRU fuse.
Make sure there is no extra strapping
which would defeat the object of the
HRU.

Rapid sinkings are more common with
motor cruisers involved in high speed
impacts when boats have been known to
sink in under 30 seconds.

A liferaft is an extremely heavy bit of kit. When you need it, it's likely to be in a hurry so stowage is very important.

VALISE PACKED RAFT

Should be stowed in a dedicated weatherproof locker directly accessible to the cockpit. A valise should not be left strapped on an exposed deck or buried deep in a locker under piles of sails and fenders!

Pros
Cheaper to buy.
Easier to move around as it has handles and a valise is lighter than a canister.
Less likely to be washed overboard or stolen as it's stowed in a locker.

Cons
Not weatherproof so contents may be damaged by water if left exposed.
Harder to deploy as it requires lifting out of a locker.
Can't be used with an HRU.

You can now get a vacuum packed valise that can be stowed on deck. They are expensive to service, but popular for racing as they are lightweight.

LIFERAFT STOWAGE

CANISTER PACKED RAFT

Weatherproof and heavy, so should be stored on chocks or a cradle on deck or on a bracket on the transom of larger craft. When siting chocks be careful not to block essential drain holes. The raft needs to breath, collected water will prevent this.

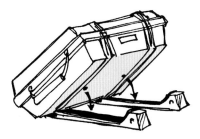

Pros
Accessible so easily deployed.
Contents protected from damage.
Can be used with an HRU.

Cons
More likely to be stolen or washed off deck.
More expensive to buy.
Prone to damage from crew standing/sitting on it.

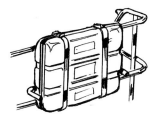

Transom hung rafts in dedicated brackets are probably the best option. They are easy to release, secure and out of the way.

Don't sit or step on the raft, this may break the seal between the two shells and let in water.

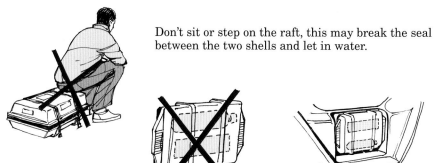

If you want to stow your raft vertically it must be specially packed, otherwise the weight of the cylinder may damage the raft and contents and the drain holes will be in the wrong place. The service centre can repack your raft for vertical stowage at the next annual service.

LIFERAFT EQUIPMENT

Safety knife - usually found in small sheath by the entrance. Use to cut painter as close to the yacht as possible, the line may be useful later.

Paddles - essential for moving clear of a burning yacht and very useful for manoeuvring to pick up survivors from the water.

Sea anchor - deploy immediately you are clear of the stricken vessel. It increases stability and reduces drift. Can be retrieved if progress to leeward is desirable.

Rescue quoit and 30m line.

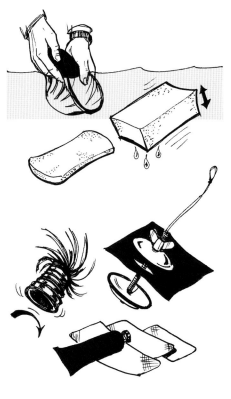

Bailer - in smaller rafts it is often no better than a shower cap. Boots are much more effective but are a last resort as you will suffer heat loss if they are removed. It's extremely difficult to bail with the doorway closed, a dinghy stirrup pump is very effective. Pack one in the grab bag.

Sponge (2) - use one to help dry out the raft, the other should be kept uncontaminated and used to collect drinking water by wiping condensation from inside the raft canopy.

Leak stoppers (set) - these rubber threaded bungs are surprisingly effective for plugging air holes in sponsons.

Repair kit - you need a perfectly calm dry day before you can use this as you need to deflate the tube and dry it before applying the patch.

LIFERAFT EQUIPMENT

Pump - inflating the floor is a long, hard job but worth doing for the extra insulation. Avoid pumping water into the floor.

Keep the tubes fully inflated. There is always some air loss through pressure release valves, punctures, daily expansion and contraction of air and buffeting by waves.

Tie the pump in. Lose it and you'll need to keep the tubes topped up by mouth.

Flares - probably one of the most important pieces of equipment on the liferaft. Make sure you are familiar with the triggering methods and use of different types. Keep them dry and do not use unless you have to.

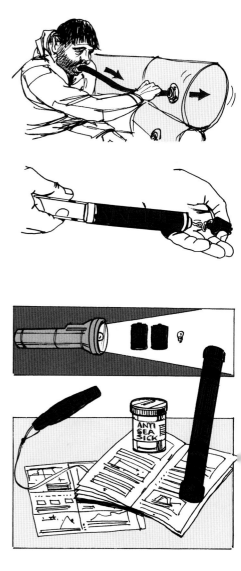

Torch - essential if there are casualties and for repairs or signalling after dark. (Includes spare batteries and bulbs).

Signal card - will help you understand communications from rescuers.

Instruction leaflet - information varies tremendously from raft to raft. Essentially a drill prompt sheet.

Anti-seasick tablets - should be issued as soon as possible.

Whistle - more effective than shouting.

LIFERAFT EQUIPMENT

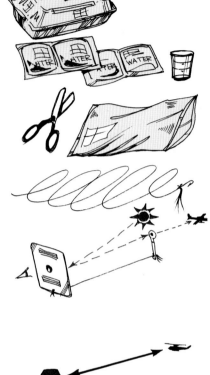

First aid kit

Water - only half a litre per person in sachets. Supplement this in the grab bag. (N.B. None in SOLAS B or ORC equipment packs)

Drinking cup

Scissors
Plastic bags - use as sick bags, for protecting burns or injuries, and keeping things dry.

Fishing kit - you must have extra water to aid digestion of fish otherwise you may be worse off. It is possible to obtain water by sucking fluids from the bones and eyes of larger fish.

Heliograph (signalling mirror) - you can also use an ordinary mirror or piece of shiny metal.

Radar reflector - fitted under a net or on a telescopic pole.

TPAs (2) - Thermal Protective Aids are good for reducing heat loss.

Food - type varies with the manufacturer. 10,000 kilo joules per person

GRAB BAG CONTENTS

The grab bag is designed to supplement the contents of a liferaft, ideally it should float and be watertight. The contents should be in waterproof packaging which can be opened with cold wet fingers.

The list of recommended contents for the grab bag for RORC/ORC liferafts appears in the Appendix.

EPIRB - if you have one, make sure it's in the liferaft with you.

Handheld VHF - for communicating with the rescue services.

GPS - so you can give the rescue services your position.

Mobile phone - useful if you are close to land and don't have a handheld VHF but remember the rescue services can't get a position fix on it.

Flares are one of the most important items in the grab bag. You must be familliar with the operating instructions, don't wait until an emergency to read the instructions.

GRAB BAG CONTENTS

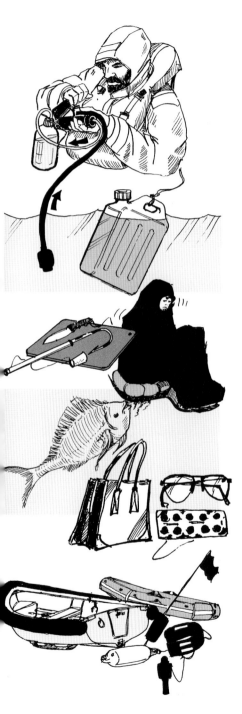

OTHER IDEAS FOR THE GRAB BAG

Desalinator, useful for turning sea water into drinking water but very expensive.

Camera flash An effective signalling device for attracting attention.

SART.

Water should be carried in several small containers to protect the whole supply from contamination. Leave an air gap so they float.

Extra TPAs, plastic bags, bin liners or an old wetsuit to help preserve body heat.

Sharp knife and sharpening stone.

Gaff.

Extra padding will protect you from buffeting by large fish feeding on small fish sheltering under the liferaft.

Documents, passport and money.

Spare spectacles.

Medication for existing conditions such as heart problems, asthma etc.

Shipping lane/wind charts.

First aid kit.

Note paper, pens, pencils

ABANDONING SHIP

Don't abandon ship unless you have done everything to save the vessel – it is your best liferaft. Even if it appears to be full of water it may stay afloat for a long time.

Yachts have been saved by emptying the water tanks, so turning them into buoyancy tanks, or disconnecting the raw water feed, closing the seacock and using the engine to pump out the bilge via the cooling system.

DRILLS FOR ABANDONING SHIP

Prior to abandonment

1. Initiate EPIRB. Make distress call.
2. Fire parachute rockets if someone is likely to be within 40 miles.
3. Put on many layers of warm clothing. Extra clothing will not weigh you down - initially it will help you to float.
4. Waterproofs/oilskins increase insulation so reducing heat loss. Use an immersion suit. Keeping warm is a top priority.
5. Check everyone has donned lifejackets correctly, inflate before entering water.
6. Have a drink (non-alcoholic) and take seasickness tablets.
7. Grab bag and as many extras as you can lay your hands on. See lists of liferaft equipment and grab bag contents plus extra lifejackets, fenders, sleeping bags etc.
8. Standby to launch in case the vessel has to be abandoned rapidly.

If you manage to don a lifejacket, send a MAYDAY, trigger EPIRB and launch liferaft, you have done well, anything else is a bonus.

Never launch the liferaft earlier than you need to use it, it is impossible to hold a raft alongside in rough seas.

LAUNCHING AND ENTERING LIFERAFT

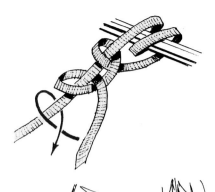

PRIOR TO LAUNCHING THE LIFERAFT

1. Check the painter is secured to a strong point.
2. Check water is clear of debris or the raft may be damaged as soon as it inflates.

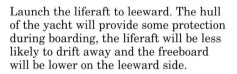

Launch the liferaft to leeward. The hull of the yacht will provide some protection during boarding, the liferaft will be less likely to drift away and the freeboard will be lower on the leeward side.

Liferafts are extremely heavy and difficult to manhandle, especially in a heavy sea. It is very difficult to lift out of the bottom of a deep locker, much easier to launch from a deck stowage.

You may need to move the raft, if there is a fire for instance. Be extremely careful you do not slip and injure yourself or lose the raft over the side.

LAUNCHING AND ENTERING LIFERAFT

LAUNCHING THE LIFERAFT

After launching, pull the painter quickly before the raft drifts away, a final tug fires the CO_2 cylinder. There will be about 25ft of line to pull out before it fires.

The raft should fully inflate in 30-60 seconds, longer in arctic conditions.

You may hear gas leaking during and shortly after inflation. This is the excess CO_2 being expelled through pressure release valves, and is normal.

It is usually preferable to deploy the raft on the lee side so the yacht offers some protection from the sea. Avoid letting the raft drift away, it may be difficult or even impossible to winch it back, leaving you with no raft.

Launched to windward the raft risks being damaged on the vessel.

If the raft inflates upside down or capsizes before you can enter it, try to right it from the vessel.

STAY OUT OF THE WATER - COLD KILLS

LAUNCHING AND ENTERING LIFERAFT

Try to climb directly into the raft from the yacht.

The fittest, strongest and heaviest person should enter the raft first to stabilise it and help others in.

Avoid jumping if at all possible, you risk injuring yourself or others already in the raft. Do not jump onto canopy. If you have to jump the maximum height is 2 metres.

REMEMBER TO BRING GRAB BAG AND EXTRAS

Leave the injured until last. Other people may land on them and make their injuries worse. If healthy people are on board they can help get casualties in. Left in the water while you struggle to get a casualty on board they may become hypothermic, resulting in two casualties.

The first people on board should sit on the windward side to minimise the risk of the liferaft being flipped over by the wind. In bad weather put your arms through the straps to avoid sliding around.

LAUNCHING AND ENTERING LIFERAFT

If you are unable to enter the liferaft
direct:

Enter the water slowly, this will reduce
cold shock.

If you jump from a height:

Check water is clear of obstructions
Hold lifejacket down with one hand
Block nose and mouth with the other
hand
Jump feet first and together
Do not look down, you are more likely to
fall forward.

In certain situations it may be prudent
to clip your safety line to the painter of
the raft and pull yourself along it until
you reach the raft.

While waiting to climb in push your arm
through the lifelines fixed around the
raft. Your hands will probably be numb
with cold. But once in contact NEVER
let go until you have boarded.

LAUNCHING AND ENTERING LIFERAFT

GETTING INTO A RAFT

It is very difficult to climb unaided into a liferaft while wearing a cumbersome lifejacket and numb with cold. All liferafts have ramps or ladders which aid entry.

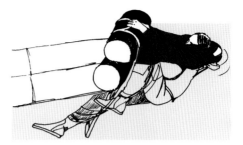

If you are alone and unable to climb into the liferaft, partially deflating your lifejacket may make boarding possible.

The skipper should look after himself first. If he becomes hypothermic, which can happen very quickly, he will not be able to provide leadership for the crew.

RESCUING SURVIVORS

Someone either side of the doorway to pull survivors in forwards is the fastest and most effective method of rescuing survivors.

Check that survivors are not laying face down in a pool of water on the raft floor.

Pulling casualties in backwards using positive buoyancy from dunking is slow and difficult.

GET EVERYONE OUT OF THE WATER FAST!

LAUNCHING AND ENTERING LIFERAFT

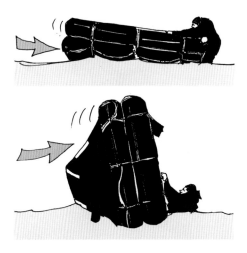

RIGHTING A CAPSIZED RAFT

Swim round to where the bottle is, reach up to the straps on the bottom of the raft, lean back using your knees as a fulcrum and pull the raft over on top of you. Much easier if you get the wind underneath the raft as you begin to lift it.

DON'T LET GO.
If the wind catches an empty raft it will be blown away much faster than you can swim.

There may be sufficient air trapped underneath for you to breathe.

Turn onto your back and pull yourself out, being careful not to hit your head on the cylinder.

Don't try to swim out face down, the buoyancy in your lifejacket will trap you against the floor of the raft.

INITIAL ACTIONS

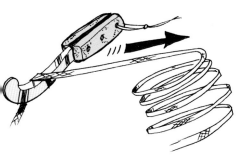

Cut the painter using the safety knife stowed near the entrance to the liferaft to cut the painter as close to the point of attachment to the vessel as possible. Pull in painter quickly, it may be useful later. Paddle clear of sinking vessel which may damage the raft. Pick up other survivors in the water.

Stream the sea anchor as soon as you're clear of the vessel. It greatly improves stability and reduces drift so keeping you in the area where the rescuers will be searching. It will also keep the entrance away from the prevailing wind and waves.

Close the raft entrance to keep ou cold and wet and keep in warmth. Always use slip knots on the doorway. Open the doorway every 20 minutes to allow fresh air in. If the raft tubes vent inside the CO_2 will need to escape.

Maintain the security of the raft by checking for leaks and bailing out.

Remember -

CUT the painter
STREAM the anchor
CLOSE the door
MAINTAIN the raft.

SECONDARY ACTIONS

WHAT TO DO NEXT

Open Liferaft Pack. Issue seasickness pills. Everyone must take them, even the hardiest of sailors are likely to be sick inside a raft. Once someone is seasick everyone else is likely to be affected. Not only will seasickness cause a physical and psychological low ebb but valuable body heat and fluid will be lost.

Bail out. This may be easier said than done. Some bailers resemble a small shower cap and you may be better off using your boots or some other container you have salvaged. Use the portable bilge pump in the grab bag. Try and keep one of your sponges uncontaminated by sea water. Use it to mop up condensation from inside the canopy for drinking.

Apply first aid to anyone requiring it. Everyone is likely to be suffering from varying degrees of hypothermia and shock in addition to injuries.

Wring out wet clothing and huddle together for warmth. Your main heat loss is by conduction through the raft floor. Insulate against this by inflating the floor, sit on your lifejackets (conditions permitting), fenders, bunk cushions, anything you may have salvaged.

In SOLAS A/B equipment packs there are two TPAs. Use thick plastic bags/builders plastic to wrap yourself in, it has excellent thermal insulating properties.

KEEP YOUR HEAD WARM.

SECONDARY ACTIONS

Read the survival notes in the instruction booklet to refresh your memory.

Check for leaks, top up with pump if necessary. Repair kits will only work if you can dry the area.

A leader, who may not be the skipper, will emerge. It may be the fittest person with the most knowledge. Their job is to make sure everyone believes they are going to be rescued.
It is important that everyone works as a team to increase the chances of survival and keep each other's morale up.

The will to survive is paramount.

Establish a routine as soon as possible. If you have enough crew put two people on watch for between 20 minutes and 2 hours depending on weather conditions.

Outside watch should keep a lookout for ships, aircraft, other survivors and dangers. They must be fully briefed on signalling with parachute rockets, heliograph and VHF.

Inside watch should keep the raft inflated, treat casualties, collect water, bail out etc.

SECONDARY ACTIONS

Sharp objects should be collected to prevent accidental damage to the liferaft, or to prevent someone using it as a potential weapon when things get a bit tight.

Look after the hand held VHF, EPIRB and flares, they are probably your best means of location by rescuers. Switch off the light during the day. It may seem very dim, but to an SAR helicopter's light intensifying equipment it will stand out for miles. SOLAS rafts have a radar reflector, wetting the canopy may also increase the radar detection range. Congregating rafts will increase the visibility to SAR.

To avoid urine retention which could have serious consequences later, urinate within two hours of boarding. You cannot reabsorb urine from the bladder so it won't increase your rate of dehydration. Try to get rid of urine overboard, and avoid urinating in your clothes as cross infection could cause problems later.

A bowel movement is not uncommon. You will probably not need to do it again as you are not ingesting food or fluid.

PROTECTION

In Northern European waters the cold is your greatest enemy. If you have lost the boat, the liferaft is designed to help save you from drowning and reduce heat loss from wind chill. The greatest heat loss is from conduction through the floor of the raft. Inflating the liferaft floor, sitting on lifejackets, fenders, bunk cushions or anything you may have salvaged, will help reduce this source of heat loss.

You lose a lot of heat through your head - pull up your hood.

Thermal protective aids (TPA's), effectively large polythene bags, have good thermal insulating properties. Metal foil sheets, often sold as "Space Blankets", are not effective in a marine environment because they do not prevent heat loss by conduction.

Survival suits are designed for extreme conditions and are the best form of protection against cold. They are bulky, expensive, and awkward to put on, particularly in a hurry in a confined space. Hence they are seldom carried on yachts.

37

WATER AND FOOD RATIONING

Ideally no food or water should be taken in the first twenty-four hours except by children or conscious casualties. If you only have the minimum water ration, the drill, after twenty-four hours, is half a litre per person per day. Take a third of a ration at sunrise, a third at midday and a third at sunset.

When drinking water, keep it in your mouth for as long as possible to moisten the membranes. Don't ration water if you have plenty and start collecting rainwater from the outset.

It is vital for morale that food and water are seen to be issued fairly. You can live for 7-10 days without water as long as there has been no excessive fluid loss, and for 20-30 days without food.

In Northern European waters you are unlikely to be adrift for much more than 48 hours before you are rescued. Your greatest enemies are hypothermia and drowning, not dehydration or starvation.

DO NOT drink urine. DO NOT drink sea water, even in a diluted state. Death has been found to occur faster if you drink salt water rather than taking nothing at all.

Drink collected rainwater first, bottled water will stay fresh longer than rainwater.

Avoid eating protein - based food such as fish or meat because digesting them uses up vital body fluid. Sugars and carbohydrates are better.

LONG TERM SURVIVAL TECHNIQUES

The will to live, paramount if you are to survive, depends on a positive mental attitude. Fear, panic and despair will all undermine it. Knowledge of survival techniques and confidence in equipment will help you remain calm and positive.

Rest as much as you can, fatigue and exhaustion will increase depression. When not asleep or resting, keep busy with routine raft duties.

Long term survival techniques revolve around collecting rainwater, fishing, keeping the raft inflated/repaired and watch keeping.

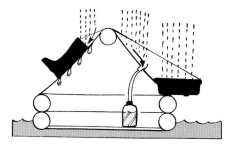

COLLECT RAINWATER AT EVERY OPPORTUNITY

Most liferafts have a small rain catchment system, so it is important to improvise. As the rain clouds approach, wash down the canopy and rinse containers with fresh seawater to clear away concentrated salt crystals. Use the first downpour as a final rinse before collecting water.

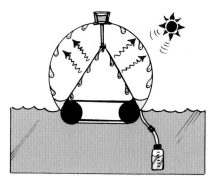

Wipe down condensation on the inside of the canopy with an uncontaminated sponge.

A solar still is difficult to get hold of and only produces between 0.75 and 1 litre of fresh water per day.

However it will run for up to two months and is excellent for morale.

A desalinator or water purifier pump will remove 98% of salt from sea water. Although they are very effective, producing a gallon of fresh water per hour, it is physically hard work and they are extremely expensive.

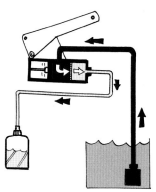

LONG TERM SURVIVAL TECHNIQUES

Fish have been caught by placing bait at the end of a sock. Gaffs and spears are more effective than a line and hooks.

Turtle blood can be used as fluid replacement if drunk within 30 seconds of being extracted, i.e. before it congeals. If the only fluid you have is brackish water, it may be safer to administer it by enema to prevent the risk of stomach upsets.

Some form of cutting board is useful and can be improvised from a flare container or salvaged flotsom.

Sea birds have been caught using fishing line. Fluid can be extracted from large fish by sucking their bones and eyes.

LONG TERM SURVIVAL TECHNIQUES

In northern waters keeping warm is the most difficult thing, but in the tropics where a lot of long distance sailing is done, staying cool is a problem.

Wet the canopy and stay out of the sun, keep your clothes damp. Regularly rinse your clothes in the sea to prevent a build-up of salt crystals which increase the effects of chafe and exacerbates sores.

If you were on a yacht with more than one liferaft, congregate rafts to increase their chance of being spotted. Spread out between rafts so everyone has as much room as possible in warm climes, huddle together in cold.

In hot weather re-attach the sea anchor to the door side so you will catch the maximum breeze.

Don't get into the water to cool down, you may not be able to get back into the raft.

RESCUE BY LIFEBOAT

If you are rescued by a lifeboat you may
see its flashing blue light before the
crew spots you. If you've got a portable
VHF talk him in. Use nautical terms not
clock notation: 'I'm on your port bow 1/2
a mile ...' etc.

Tell him if there are casualties, whether
there are any children, the state of
everyone on board, whether they are
concussed, injured, unconscious, etc.

Leave as much of the liferaft painter
intact as possible when you abandon
ship. When the lifeboat arrives show the
coxswain that you have a painter
attached to your liferaft. He can use it
to secure the raft alongside during the
rescue.

The lifeboat will either approach head
or stern to wind to avoid becoming
entangled with the sea anchor.

RESCUE BY HELICOPTER

If you are rescued by helicopter you may see him before he spots you. If so, guide him in with a portable VHF if you have one - 'We are lying to your 3 o'clock...'.

Orange smoke or hand held flares will help pinpoint your position.

Avoid firing parachute flares. If you have nothing else, and think you have not been spotted, fire away from the helicopter. You don't want your rescuers down in the water with you.

Listen to instructions and do as the helicopter crew ask. They are highly trained and know what they are doing. Tell them of the conditions of casualties, are they concussed, injured, unconscious etc. Remember their condition before the helicopter appeared, the euphoria of imminent rescue can mask symptoms.

Don't all crowd to one side of the liferaft, the downdraught from the helicopter may blow the raft over.

Helicopters usually lower a winch man into the raft where he will attach any casualties to a strop or stretcher. Earth the line from the helicopter by allowing it to touch the water before taking hold of it.

If the helicopter is using a "highline", hang onto the line when casualties are being winched up, this will prevent them spinning in the downdraught. Survivors will often be lifted in pairs for speed.

When you are being lifted don't raise your arms, the strop may slip off.

RESCUE BY SHIP

If you are rescued by a large commercial ship, the crew may have no idea of how to go about getting you out of the sea. It is important to communicate with them. Crew 90ft up on deck will have little appreciation of what the sea state is like on a small vessel.

Numb with cold and exhausted, you are unlikely to be able to climb a ship's ladder. Be careful that the euphoria of rescue doesn't make you think you can - you may get 10ft up only to fall back into the sea and drown.

Beware, a ducted propeller could suck you in from anywhere 1/3 way aft of the ship.

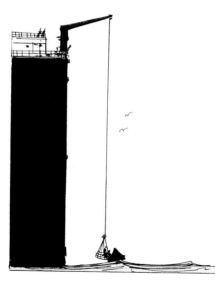

The best thing for a large vessel is to stand off and lower a rescue tender, or better still, a cargo net and get everyone in at once.

You will survive longer if you :

Wear a lifejacket.
Put on several layers of clothes followed by your oilskins. This will act as a kind of wetsuit and keep you warm.
Don't kick off your boots they will help keep you warm.
Unless help is close by do not swim. Conserve heat in the HELP position (Heat Escape Lessening Posture). Cross legs (bent knees will make you unstable). Tuck elbows in holding lifejacket down and covering face with hands. In this position your legs act as a drogue keeping you facing the wind.

Pull spray hood (if fitted) across. After two minutes, swim on your back using only your legs. Using your arms will speed up the onset of hypothermia.

Heat loss in water is twenty-six times greater than in air. Staying still in the HELP position or in the HUDDLE reduces water flow across the body so increasing your survival time.

The HUDDLE, two or more people lock arms and face each other. It improves morale, helps the survival of weaker members of the group and increases your chances of being spotted by the SAR services.

Always stay together, swim as a group, or send a strong swimmer ahead connected to the group by the line.

Swimming is not recommended in cold water as it will speed up the onset of hypothermia.

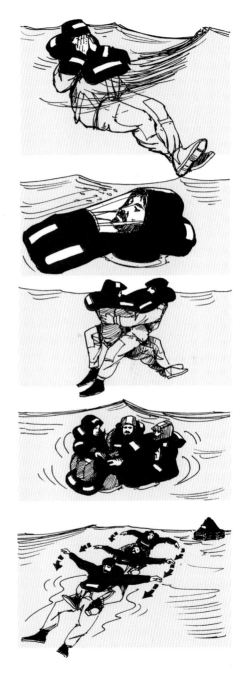

SURVIVAL IN COLD WATER

For more general information on diagnosis and treatment of casualties refer to the St. Johns First Aid Book.

DROWNING

The risk of drowning is reduced if you are wearing a good lifejacket with a hood. Avoid swimming as you will quickly become breathless and the cold will stiffen up the limbs. Get into HELP or HUDDLE position if you can't get out of the water.

Symptoms - Breathing has stopped or is very shallow, blue lips, bluish pallor, froth around the lips and nostrils. If conscious the patient may be complaining of chest pain and coughing.

Treatment - You need to get air into the lungs by EAR (Expired Air Resuscitation) as quickly as possible.

Don't try to expel water from lungs, this will happen automatically when the casualty starts breathing.

SECONDARY DROWNING

A casualty who has inhaled a small amount of dirty water may suffer secondary drowning. The lung reacts by releasing fluid from the blood into the lungs. It is very rare.

Symptoms - Severe chest pain and coughing (possibly blood), it is likely to manifest itself within 12 hours of the incident. If you suspect anything always seek medical attention.

Treatment - must be hospitalised and given oxygen.

HEART ATTACK

Do not attempt cardiac massage in a raft unless it has a wooden floor. Beware, casualties are probably suffering from hypothermia as well. The heart might be beating but very weakly. In this case cardiac massage might do more harm than good.

HYPOTHERMIA

Normal core body temperature is 37°C, hypothermia occurs when body temperature drops to 35°C.

You can become hypothermic in water up to 24°C. Around the UK the water temperature varies between 5°C and 18°C and even in the Mediterranean in summer the water rarely gets above 26°C.

In the summer your survival time with clothing and lifejacket is between two and nine hours. In winter it is from minutes to two hours. The rate of heat loss is twenty-six times greater in water than in air.

STAGE 1

When the water first hits your face you hold your breath, blood circulation shuts down and heart rate slows - this is called the Diving Reflex.

Within seconds cold shock takes over. You experience the pain of cold water, your breathing rate increases from around 10 to 60 breaths a minute (hyperventilation). External blood vessels shut down causing blood pressure to shoot up. All this increases the chances of suffering a stroke or heart attack.

Protecting against cold shock. Wear protective clothing and, if possible, enter the water slowly. The more used to the cold, and the fitter you are, the better your chances of surviving. Do not try to swim. Stay in Help/Huddle position until your breathing rate has settled.

SURVIVAL IN COLD WATER

STAGE 2

Short term immersion symptoms develop after anywhere between three and thirty minutes. Heart and breathing rates decrease and shivering increases. Even strong swimmers may only manage 100 metres before collapsing and drowning. This emphasises the importance of wearing a lifejacket.

If help is at hand and you are going to be rescued in under an hour, swim on your back, kicking your legs. Avoid using your arms, it increases the rate of heat loss. Otherwise stay in the HELP position ideally wearing a face visor, your legs will act as a sea anchor and you will be facing the weather.

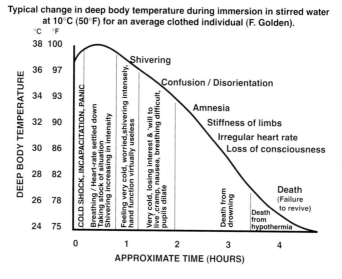

Typical change in deep body temperature during immersion in stirred water at 10°C (50°F) for an average clothed individual (F. Golden).

STAGE 3

Long term immersion symptoms develop after 30 minutes. Hypothermia sets in as core temperature drops from 37°C to 35°C. The casualty will feel very cold, the body becomes numb, intense shivering may cease as the muscles become cramped and rigid. Speech becomes slurred, nausea sets in and behaviour becomes irrational. Unconsciousness occurs, heart and breathing rates decrease and pupils dilate.

Casualty is at risk of heart failure when body temperature drops below 30°C.

Protection
Layers of clothing and waterproofs or a survival suit will prolong survival time. Fatigue, injury and the intake of alcohol will all reduce survival time.

TREATMENT OF HYPOTHERMIA

Hypothermia is extremely difficult to treat in a
survival situation but the most important thing
is to stop any further heat loss and to encourage
an increase in core body temperature.

Treatment
Remove wet clothing if conscious and co-
operative.
Insulate by wrapping in blankets and sleeping
bags and wrap in plastic, leaving the face
exposed. Ensure that the casualty is well
insulated underneath.

The metabolic heat produced by the internal organs
will slowly warm the body from the inside. Once the
air inside the plastic has reached 100% humidity
(saturation point) further heat loss will be greatly
reduced.

Buddy system is also a good way to maintain each
other's body heat.

Warm drinks, which contain about 60 calories of heat,
can be given to a conscious casualty. A hypothermic
person may have lost some 2000 calories of heat. The
emphasis should be on stopping further heat loss and
giving the body a chance to warm up from the inside.

Handle the unconscious hypothermic very carefully, rough handling can cause
collapse and even death.

DO NOT
Give alcohol
Use hot water bottles
Massage/rub areas
Handle roughly
Administer fluid to
semi/unconcious person.

Space Blankets only reflect radiated heat. When you're hypothermic heat loss is
mainly by conduction for which a space blanket is useless.

Rewarming - Unless you know what you are doing, active rewarming is not
recommended. It's unlikely to be possible in a liferaft or small yacht.

SURVIVAL IN COLD WATER

NORMAL   HYPOTHERMIC

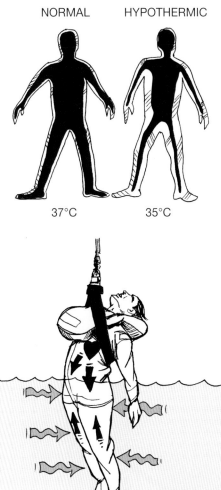

37°C   35°C

POST RESCUE COLLAPSE

When you get cold the body restricts blood flow to the skin so reducing heat loss and concentrating the same volume of blood in the vital organs.

Research and observations from SAR Lee on Solent helicopter show that the hydrostatic squeeze of the water on an immersion casualty is helping support the circulation. If the casualty is lifted vertically out of the water the blood drains from the head and a drop in blood pressure at the heart can result in a heart attack.

Casualties should if possible be lifted using a two strop method, basket or stretcher technique.

SHOCK

Shock is extremely serious, even fatal and can have a number of causes, including:

Injury - internal or external bleeding
Burns
Severe vomiting/diarrhoea
Fear/pain/traumatic experience

The result is a reduced blood flow carrying oxygen to the vital organs. Unnecessary movement can cause fainting and even heart failure.
Beware of delayed shock. A man overboard casualty may assure his rescuers that he is perfectly okay, and to all intents and purposes he is. However, some 20-60 minutes later he may go into shock.

Symptoms
Casualty becomes pale or grey
Skin is cold, moist with sweat (difficult to diagnose having just climbed out of a cold sea)
Feels weak/faint
Nauseous
Pulse is weak and rapid
Breathing becomes shallow and rapid, may be gasping
Complains of thirst
May lapse into unconsciousness

Treatment
Most of the crew are likely to be suffering from varying degrees of shock and there is probably very little you can do in a liferaft.

1. Treat any obvious cause such as external bleeding
2. Reassure the casualty
3. Lie him down with his head to one side to avoid danger of choking if he vomits
4. Raise the legs
5. Loosen clothing
6. Keep him warm
7. Moisten lips with water but do not give anything to drink/eat. Do not apply hot water bottles, it can cause circulation collapse.
8. If he becomes unconscious and stops breathing, complete ABC of resuscitation.

SURVIVAL IN COLD WATER

FROSTBITE

The lookout in the liferaft is the most susceptible to frostbite, a condition where local tissue is frozen, usually fingers, toes, ears and nose.

Prevention
Protection from the elements and exercise and massage in early stages will prevent the onset of cold injury.

Symptoms
The area becomes pale then white, a mottled blue colour and finally bluey black. The affected area swells as fluid escapes from damaged cells, and feeling is lost.

Treatment
Raise affected area
Remove constricting garments
Dry area
Warm by placing in armpit, groin or between warm hands
Do not massage
Do not burst blisters
Do not apply pressure

IMMERSION FOOT

If feet are cold and wet for long periods a condition called Immersion Foot can result.

Symptoms
Feet become white as local circulation is reduced causing swelling of tissues and numbness.

Treatment
Dry feet
Rapid rewarming
Gentle exercise
Give warm drinks

As the foot warms up it will be painful.

HEAT EXHAUSTION

A condition caused by loss of water and salt from the body usually as a result of physical exercise in a hot, moist environment.

Symptoms
The casualty will complain of fatigue, headache, dizziness, nausea, perhaps even vomiting and muscular cramps. The skin will be cold, pale and clammy, the pulse weak and rapid, breathing fast and shallow. The casualty may faint.

Treatment
Remove from direct heat and vent the liferaft.
Sponge down body.
Give sips of cold water with a little salt.

HEAT STROKE

A condition caused by prolonged exposure to extreme heat or high humidity, the body temperature rises due to inability to lose heat through sweating.

Symptoms
Similar to heat exhaustion except that the skin will look flushed and dry, pulse is rapid and strong and breathing full and rapid.

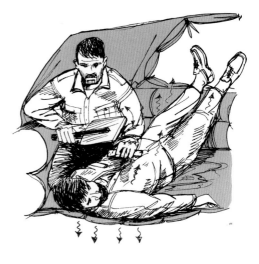

Treatment
Sponge down body.
Give frequent sips of cool slightly salted drinks.
Expose to wind chill.

APPENDIX 1

LIFERAFT EQUIPMENT PACKS

A variety of different equipment packs are available, to specifications set by authorities such as the Department of Transport and Offshore Racing Council. These may be supplemented by 'Grab bags' containing additional equipment, stowed separately from the liferaft but intended to be taken into the liferaft by the crew.

It is possible to mix and match liferafts and equipment packs and this can be a cause of confusion. For instance, it is possible to have an ORC liferaft fitted with a DoT equipment pack and it is sometimes, wrongly, thought that this constitutes a 'DoT approved liferaft'. It does not, the basic liferaft is still an ORC liferaft.

DoT EQUIPMENT PACKS (For liferafts up to 12 persons capacity)

SOLAS B PACK (RAFTS UP TO 12 PERSONS CAPACITY)

Bailer
Sponges (2)
Leakstoppers (set)
Pump
Repair Kit
Buoyant Paddles (2)
Signal card
Instruction leaflets (survival and immediate action)
Torch + spare batteries and bulb
Anti-seasickness tablets (6/person)
Rescue line and quoit
Safety knife
Sea anchor (2)
First aid kit
Sick bag (1/person)
Whistle
Red parachute flares (2)
Red handheld flares (3)
Buoyant orange smoke

Heliograph
Radar reflector
Thermal protective aids (2)

SOLAS A PACK

In addition to the contents of the SOLAS B PACK it has:

Fishing kit
Red parachute flares (2)
Red handheld flares (3)
Orange smoke
Water (0.5 litre per person)
Graduated drinking vessel
Non-thirst provoking rations, minimum of 10,000 kilo joules per person
Tin opener

ORC EQUIPMENT PACKS

EQUIPMENT FITTED IN THE RAFT

Bailer
Red handheld flares (3)
Sponges (2)
Torch, spare batteries and bulb
Leak stoppers (set)
Pump
Anti-seasickness tablets (6 per person)
Repair kit (can only be used in calm, dry conditions)
Paddles (2)
Whistle
Signal card
Safety knife
Instruction leaflet
Sea anchor
Rescue quoit and 30m of floating line

ADDITIONAL EQUIPMENT IN GRAB BAG

Sea anchor and line (spare)
Tin openers (2)
Handheld waterproof VHF
EPIRB
First aid kit
Cyalume sticks (2) or throwable floating lamps (2)
Signalling mirror
Whistle
Water (min. 0.5 litre per person)
Graduated plastic drinking vessel
Non thirst provoking rations and barley sugars
Nylon string
Anti-seasickness pills
Red parachute flares (2)
Red handheld flares (3)

ALTERNATIVE GRAB BAG

This alternative grab bag list is specified by the DoT for yachts certficated for commercial use carrying ORC liferafts.

Second sea anchor and line
First aid kit
One daylight signalling mirror
One signalling whistle
One radar reflector
Two red parachute flares
Three red hand held flares
One buoyant smoke signal
One thermal protective aid for each person on board.
One copy of the illustrated table of life-saving signals (SOLAS No.2)

APPENDIX 2

RYA/DoT BASIC SEA SURVIVAL FOR SMALL CRAFT – COURSE SYLLABUS

PART 1 - Preparation for Sea Survival

Survival difficulties
Survival requirements
Equipment available
Training drills and their importance
Actions prior to abandonment

PART 2 - Lifejackets and Liferafts

Lifejackets -
  design and construction
  BS 3595, CEN
  correct donning procedure
  purpose and use of lifejackets
  entering the water from a height
Safety Harness -
  design and construction BS 4224
  purpose and use
  securing arrangements
Liferafts -
  standards DoT, SOLAS and ORC
  stowage and containment onboard
  design and construction
  launching a deck stowed liferaft
  abandoning the vessel
  righting a capsized liferaft
  helping injured persons onboard
  liferaft equipment
  initial actions to be taken in a
  liferaft

PART 3 - Practical Wet Drill

Liferaft launching
Boarding dry and wet
Jumping from the poolside or from 1m
board
Methods to increase chances of survival
once in water
Helping injured persons
Raft capsize drill
Final abandonment exercise

PART 4 - Principles of Survival

Protection -
  Cold conditions
  signs and symptoms of
  hypothermia
  methods of treatment for
  hypothermia victims
  Hot Conditions
  sunburn, heat exhaustion and
  heatstroke - signs and symptoms
  methods of treatment
Location
  Survival routines to aid location
  correct use of pyrotechnics
  use of other locational aids
Water
  Water rationing procedures
  Problems related to dehydration
  and preventative measures
  collection of water
Food
  Food rationing
  Sources of food
Survival Craft Ailments
  Frostbite and immersion foot
  Urine retention
  Constipation
  Salt water boils etc.
  Medical aspects of survival
  Secondary actions
  Subsequent actions
  Raft management

PART 5 Search and Rescue

Rescue by helicopter or vessel
Role of HM Coastguard
UK and International SAR Organisation
Other services.